Mute

Also by the author

[Exeunt.]

Ironhood

Animals Out-There W-i-l-d

Far from Atlantis

Chlorophyll

Lunafly

once upon a twin

Bokeh Focus

A Babble of Objects

The Kiss of Walt Whitman Still on My Lips

How to Kill Poetry

Road Work Ahead

This Way to the Acorns

St. Michael's Fall

Praise for the original edition of <u>Mute</u>

Luczak explores the conflicts and collisions with the hearing world as an unavoidable part of a Deaf person's everyday navigation, and he does so with sensitivity though he's honest about the frustrations and challenges to one's patience. In the poem "Waiting for You to Learn Sign Language," there's even a bit of an incentive: "Love, open your hands. You are a corked geyser." Being Deaf offers this gay poet (and his beloved) access to a unique communication and landscape of tactile metaphors that enriches the poetry on the page.

But of deeper relevance is his poetic skill, the ease with which he operates with rhyme (see the villanelle "Repetitions" and the couplet sonnet "The Elegist") and the transcendent, transformative tone of his message to those who take language (in any of its manifestations) for granted.

—Rigoberto González, *Lambda Literary Review*

I'll be honest: The opening poem of *Mute* entitled "How to Fall for a Deaf Man" is so achingly beautiful that it actually made me cry. That's no easy feat, yet Luczak's lines are so tender and insightful that they cut to the heart of the matter and invite you to read and re-read them, over and over. ... His words transgress the hearing world, laying bare its prejudices. There is an undeniable sorrow here, an achingly haunted world that Luczak bravely guides the reader through, one filled with moments of blistering love and undeniable mystery. Perfect for lovers of language.

—Scott-Patrick Mitchell, *Out in Perth*

Sexual politics rears its head in Raymond Luczak's wonderful *Mute*, exploring themes that elucidate what it's like to walk between the hearing and Deaf worlds. Luczak negotiates this path between spheres with ease, his language reflecting the pain and experience that purchased his facility ("Waiting for You to Learn Sign Language," "One Day When I Lose My Speech") and inform those pieces that are not about deafness at all ("Night Stroll in Washington D.C.," "The Loom"). Luczak is a powerful poet whose work is as important as it is beautiful.

—Jerry Wheeler, *Out in Print*

Beautiful and elegant, Luczak's poetry hits the reader with a slap across the face.

—Amos Lassen, who listed *Mute* as the third best book of 2010

Mute is a book about communication—or the possibility of it. Using print as a medium, Luczak tries to negotiate that terrain in which spoken language is not an option (or is, at best, a very poor one) and the written word will not suffice.

Unlike poets whose major purpose in writing is to "express themselves," Luczak has constituency for whom he is speaking. Thus, his work is not mute at all. This is not to say that Luczak is a mouthpiece for either the Deaf or gay communities. His life and poetry is much too idiosyncratic for that. He does, however, give readers a pictures of a slice of society, the Deaf gay culture, that they are not likely to encounter in many other volumes of poetry. As this body of literature grows, *Mute* is likely to have an important place in it.

—Michael Northen, *Wordgathering*

Mute
The Fifteenth Anniversary Edition

Raymond Luczak

Handtype Press
Minneapolis, MN

Mute: The Fifteenth Anniversary Edition
Original copyright © 2010 by Raymond Luczak.
Copyright © 2025 by Raymond Luczak.

The original edition of *Mute* was published by A Midsummer Night's Press.

This second edition includes thirteen new poems: "Guesswork," "Hands of Moon," "Murmurings," "In the Pawnshop," "Food for Thought," "A Friendship Never Meant," "Blueprinted," "1,549 Miles Away," "Uncloseting, 1984," "In Elephant Walk, 1994," "The Purpose of Astronomy," "Couplets," and "Mumbles." The poem "A Vow" from the original edition has been omitted.

Cover design: Mona Z. Kraculdy
Cover photograph: Raymond Luczak

All rights reserved. No part of this book can be reproduced in any form without written permission. Please address inquiries to the publisher:

Handtype Press
PO Box 3941
Minneapolis, MN 55403-0941
Email: handtype@gmail.com
Online: handtype.com

ISBN: 978-1-941960-19-6
Library of Congress Control Number: 2025946740

Printed in the United States of America

in memory of these glorious Deaf men

Alan R. Barwiolek
William Bradley
Mark Branson
William D. Byrd
John "Buzzy" Bautista Conterio
Samuel Edwards
Michael Eisele
Ronald A. Emrich
Samuel Feliciano
Michael P. Felts
Jack Leo Fennell
John R. Flynn
Gerry Garrison
Bruce Michael Mackintosh Hlibok
Ernest Hoffmann
Rodney Jamison
Thomas Kane
Jerry Glynn Koonce II
J. Charlie McKinney
Cagney Savoy Perkins
Olgar Schroeder
Tommy Saavedra
Edward Schwartz
James Thomas Sharer
Robert Louis Sisco
Pedro Solis
James S. Tola
Clayton L. Valli
Mike White
Guy Charles Wonder III

I remain forever orphaned

Contents

Unsilencing *Mute*: A Journey i

I.

How to Fall for a Deaf Man, 2025 3
Mannequins 9
Guesswork 10
Hearing Your Voice for the First Time 11
Pitch 12
Hands of Moon 13
Repetitions 14
Instructions for Hearing Persons Desiring a Deaf Man . 15
Waiting for You to Learn Sign Language 16
One Day When I Lose My Speech 17

II.

Murmurings 21
Buddies 22
In the Pawnshop 23
Covent Garden: Men's Room, 1889 24
Food for Thought 25
Later 27
Wink 28
In June 29
Night Stroll in Washington, D.C. 31
The Loom 33

III.

The Elegist	37
Algae	38
A Friendship Never Meant	40
International Deaf Leather, 2002	42
Blueprinted	44
1,549 Miles Away	47
Uncloseting, 1984	48
In Elephant Walk, 1994	49
The Purpose of Astronomy	50
Marenisco Eyes	52
You Died Today	54

IV.

On a Bench with Him in Central Park	59
Mute	60
Homily	61
Audiological Exam	62
Gazes	63
A Wish, Unheard	64
Couplets	65
1989	66
Mumbles	73
Orphans	75

Acknowledgments	78

Unsilencing Mute: A Journey

On a cold afternoon in January 1989, the elevator doors opened to reveal a clean-shaven businessman with curly blond hair and an aquiline nose standing behind a clot of suited executives in their tight leather shoes and rouged wanna-bes in their white Reeboks at the advertising agency where I worked. With a curious smile, he looked intently at me, and he did so with so much confidence that I was caught completely off guard.

I did not know that a single gaze could possibly convey so much.

It may have been the end of just another workday at my new job, but a new era had just sparked in my life.

I was 23 years old. I had given up a $250 basement apartment with free laundry and electricity and a garage for storage space in Washington, D.C. for an uncertain future in New York City five months before. I was fortunate to have found a railroad apartment for $600 a month on India Street in Greenpoint, a predominantly Polish neighborhood in Brooklyn. To afford the rent, I found a hearing roommate to live there. In those days, nobody wanted to visit Brooklyn!

Once I found my full-time job, though, I often took off after work to wander around Manhattan in all her glory and grime, hopping from one subway line to another, and discovering flashes of smile, neon, and glitter as I walked along one block after another. Each neighborhood felt like a tiny country where I felt like a foreigner.

For days afterward, I wondered about the stranger in the elevator. Had he truly looked at *me*? Or was it all my imagination? Did he work in my building? Or was he a client who'd come there for a presentation?

In those days, secretaries weren't required to use computers because it seemed too intimidating to learn. That's where I came in: I word-processed and formatted presentations, and media buys and ROI charts on a proprietary computer system. It was a dead-end job but I typed endlessly, which later enabled me to write easily at the speed of my thoughts. (Later, when I left that job, I took a typing test at a temp agency. They were flabbergasted to see that I could type at 123 words per minute with only two errors. It was not long before secretaries—and everyone else—would be forced to use computers, too.)

The word processing department where I worked had no windows. It was centered inside the building near the elevators. There was nothing on the beige walls. Two other word processors and our supervisor talked among themselves all day long. I felt nameless while stylish men and women rushed in with their changes. Some expected me to stay there all night for their last-minute number-crunching.

For days afterward, I searched for the stranger in the hallways outside my department. I didn't see him again. I figured that he had come there for a presentation.

In the late 1980s, the AIDS epidemic was fully raging. Even though I was horny, I was absolutely terrified of having sexual encounters. There was a lot of hysteria and misunderstanding about AIDS, but one thing was clear: The diagnosis was then considered a death sentence. The off-label medications that doctors prescribed out of desperation were often toxic.

Nevertheless, my rank loneliness compelled me to seek out strangers just as needy as I was for a few moments of physical intimacy. I found them in peep booths and adult movie theaters off Times Square. I more often said no to these men whose eyes searched mine, and yet I kept returning because I needed to see that I wasn't the only one haunted by the specter of loneliness. In the anonymity of our aches and grunts, we all had the same surname.

That I managed to remain HIV-negative through those years seems like a miracle.

Then unexpectedly: there he stood. It was the end of

another workday. The stranger was waiting to board the elevator like I was. Each time we glanced at each other, our grins broadened even more. We were the only ones waiting.

Once the elevator doors closed in front of us, I immediately asked him, "What's your name?"

I couldn't understand him. He had mumbled.

I said, "Wait." I pulled out a pen and notebook from my bag and he wrote his name: *A___ R_____*.

I said my name.

We shook hands. His fingernails were neatly trimmed. The back of his hand had blond fur. His fingers felt thick inside my thin hand. It was as if I was feeling the weight of my destiny. I noted the sharp tailoring of his suit and buffed wingtips. Up until then I hadn't noticed such details among the businessmen who sardined the subway during rush hours, but there he was. I had thought I'd experienced aliveness with another man, but this was a whole other level.

I couldn't believe how beautiful A.R. was up close. His nose was slightly sprinkled with tiny freckles. He was slightly older and balding. His eyes looked so deep that I willed myself to hold my breath as if to resist drowning in them.

But what slayed me the most was his smile, full of exuberance with a hint of sexual possibility.

He said that he worked in the media research

department on my floor. I thought it incredulous that I hadn't seen him around before!

He apologized for needing to go home that evening, but he said that we should get together after work sometime.

"Sometime"? Did he really say that?

I think my heart stopped momentarily. With my throat suddenly parched, I could only nod.

As the epicenter of American theater, New York City was jam-packed with good-looking actors. It often seemed that every man I saw was good-looking, or at least took pains to look good as possibly could. They looked nothing like the federal workers I'd seen in Washington, D.C. These New Yorkers exuded a sense of swagger and confidence that I certainly did not have in spades.

I'd nurtured my self-confidence as a Deaf gay man while at Gallaudet University: I wasn't the only Deaf student there. Actually, there were approximately 2,000 of us due to the rubella baby boom in the mid-1960s.

Deaf students with hearing families shared horror stories about being shut out of their banter at mealtimes and, in doing so, bonded as a family of sorts with their new friends. American Sign Language (ASL) became a tonic that they couldn't stop imbibing. We couldn't get enough of *signing*. Sometimes we stood for hours outside the entrance to our dormitory buildings and talked happily into the wee hours.

Gallaudet gave me an infinite sense of possibility. I would no longer be a wallflower. I would no longer be ashamed about my nasal speech because I didn't need to speak. That alone liberated me. ASL, too, gave me the truest sense of family I would ever experience. ASL became not only my passport to a vibrant community but also to my own self-confidence.

Our first get-together happened spontaneously. We happened to be waiting for the elevator at the end of a workday. He asked, "What are you doing tonight?"

I said, "Nothing, really."

"Wanna go out somewhere and talk?"

I nodded.

I was totally hard in my pants.

We ambled north to Central Park. I have no idea why he'd chosen to go there, but there we were, sitting on a bench. He had loosened his tie, and a tuft of chest fur tantalized me.

He talked about his first major boyfriend. I no longer recall what he'd said; only that I hoped that I would be his *next* major boyfriend.

I don't know what I'd said that evening, but he was intrigued enough to ask if I'd be interested in attending a gay film festival happening in Midtown.

Was I ever!

We saw three films at the festival.

The first one was John Greyson's *Urinal*. Even though it was spoken in English and not captioned, I couldn't understand a word of it. (No one had taught me about self-advocacy in the hearing world, so I never thought to request captioning.) I kept cringing because it was about cruising for sex in public restrooms and fighting for the right to do so without being arrested. I had cruised for sex with strangers, but once I came out, I promptly lost interest in anonymous encounters. Here I was, sitting next to the most handsome man I had ever seen, and recalling those moments of hunger and shame in these sordid restrooms. I discreetly scanned A.R.'s face for his reactions. Had he done the same thing? Or was he still prowling here and there?

The next film was William Friedkin's *The Boys in the Band*, which was adapted from Matt Crowley's groundbreaking play. I was in for a visceral shock. These gay men, most of whom I couldn't lipread on the screen, hated each other vehemently in spite of seeming to have a bitchy ol' time at Harold's birthday party. I felt like shit afterward. These characters could not be my people!

The third film was Rainer Werner Fassbinder's *Fox and His Friends*, a German (and finally subtitled!) film that showed Fassbinder playing Fox, the main character who was willing to give up so much for love with the wrong man. That Fassbinder wasn't an attractive man playing a pathetic character made me question why the film had been made in the first place. (I didn't know that Fassbinder was an important filmmaker. I now count *Ali: Fear Eats the Soul*, *The Bitter Tears of Petra von Kant*, and *Querelle* to be among my favorites.)

During the film, though, A.R. held my hand the entire time, which filled me with a speechless joy. Yet it would take me a long time to recover from the resurrection of my own self-loathing due to those three films.

After that, we smiled at each other in the hallways. I had hoped to see him in the men's restroom on our floor, but I never did. I longed for a moment of unfiltered admission, as in saying, "Hey, let's get naked!"

Then we went out for lunch. We grabbed takeout and went past the United Nations Building where there was a plaza that overlooked East River. As we sat on a bench and ate, he told me how he loved to travel. Even though he was 32 years old, he had visited a number of countries already. Having never touched a passport, I was totally in awe. I couldn't imagine visiting a country where no one spoke English.

Of course, it had never occurred to me that with my fluency in ASL, I was already living in a foreign country of sorts.

When A.R. said that his sister worked with Deaf students at a residential school north of New York City, I was secretly thrilled because it meant that he was more receptive to the reality of me being Deaf.

"Really?" I jokingly said, "Let's see how well you can sign."

He shook his head no. "I can't sign."

"Let's try anyway."

I was stunned by how perfectly he could mimic my signs. Most beginners are sloppy with their signing, but his signs were perfect on the first try. I tried one sign after another, and he nailed them all.

My jaw must have dropped.

He merely grinned.

By then I was completely in love with him.

I invited him to attend a reading by a deaf oralist poet in Midtown. Because we had gone there after work and dinner, A.R. was still wearing his suit but with no tie. I was in my work clothes, too. I felt a mixture of pride—*Look at this hot man standing with me!*—and fear—*Would my Deaf friends and acquaintances look down on me because I had chosen to date a hearing man?*

He had never gone to a Deaf event before. I wasn't too worried, though. If he wanted to learn, it wouldn't take him long to become fluent in ASL. We sat right in the center of the audience's seats.

The event felt slightly off-kilter. The deaf oralist poet didn't sign, so she had ASL interpreters onstage. What was more unsettling was the fact that Bruce Hlibok, the acclaimed Deaf actor and playwright, happened to sit right next to me. I was in awe of him because of his accomplishments in theater.

Bruce ignored me the entire time. The same look on everyone's faces at us two was of puzzlement: They knew I was also a Deaf writer, so why was Bruce not talking to me? Even A.R. had noticed Bruce's coldness.

In hindsight, Bruce had probably felt threatened by my presence. Which was strange, considering how I was a nobody with only two poems published.

A.R. and I still got together for lunch now and then, but we didn't go out after work like before. He never explained why; I was afraid to ask.

His growing silences began to strike fear inside me. Had he lost interest in me? Had he met someone else?

I felt lost.

I still longed to get naked with him.

I wanted to ask what I'd done wrong.

Weeks of such uncertainty dragged on. How I hated that suspense from being dangled in the air!

He still smiled at me whenever we happened to see each other at work, but it was with a great stiffness.

Finally, when I was alone in my department, I called him at his desk. He had his own corner office.

I don't remember exactly what I'd said, but I might've said, "I don't know what's happened between us, but I think it's best that we don't see each other anymore."

He probably felt a huge sigh of relief.

I cried inside every time I saw him at work.

I tried to date other men. The sex was bad. I simply wasn't ready to love again.

Prior to my relocation from Brooklyn to Manhattan, I learned that Sam Edwards, a famous Deaf dancer, had died from AIDS. I was in a state of shock.

When Sam and I met in the summer of 1987, he had made it crystal clear that he was keenly interested in me. He was doing a project at Gallaudet University. Even though I found him physically attractive, his intense eyes frightened me off. Then I learned later that Buzzy Conterio had died the year before. I had crushed on Buzzy because I knew him as the only other Deaf gay man who'd also grown up in Michigan's Upper Peninsula.

The double whammy of these Deaf gay friends dying hit me hard. I wrote my first AIDS elegy "The Purpose of Astronomy," which has been restored here. Eventually I began hearing more about this or that Deaf gay friend and acquaintance dying from AIDS; it later became an unfortunate fact of my life in the 1990s.

Six months later after Sam's passing, my father unexpectedly died from a heart attack. He was 63 years old. I felt more discombobulated than ever.

So much loss in such a short period of time: How does one even begin to grieve?

I wrote. Or at least I tried.

While trying to write my first book of poems *St. Michael's Fall*, which recounted how I was not allowed to sign while mainstreamed in a Catholic school in a small town, I felt unfocused. My book in progress had a few poems that I liked, but most of them I didn't like. They clunked from self-pity. Then I attended an extraordinary workshop led by Marilyn Hacker at the Poetry Society of America. I was able to refocus on the new poems that gave *St. Michael's Fall* its structure.

But the process of writing the poems that eventually formed *Mute* felt quite different. There was no discernible narrative; no specific book in mind then. I felt unfinished with A.R. The narrative, if there was to be one, was still happening; I was feeling quite raw. I nevertheless tried to clarify matters. Ultimately they became love poems to a hearing man who would never read them.

Of course, I fantasized that my poems would rain on his chest like bombs, and that the only place he could find the shattered remains of his heart was in my arms.

In his presence, I had no spine. I didn't understand how I'd brought it all upon myself. You see, when a man doesn't speak much, others often conjecture what he must be feeling inside. The less a desired man speaks, the more the besotted speculates. That's the enduring power of silence.

With *Mute*, I was beginning to explore love in great depth as a Deaf gay man. With *St. Michael's Fall* and *This Way to the Acorns*, I didn't dare suggest homosexual desire outright; but with *Mute*, I didn't just suggest. I was coming out not just as a Deaf gay man in print but also as an artist. If I seem to be a poet noted for his intense longings, it is because it was through such yearnings for A.R. that I learned to express myself in ways that I hadn't dared a few years earlier. I was allowing myself the risk of being vulnerable and honest with myself, and all because I was so in love with a hearing man who had made me doubt everything I'd believed about myself in my four years at Gallaudet.

I was no longer confident. I was a freak with a nasal voice filled with missing consonants. I was too skinny and too hairy; either quality didn't seem to be a plus in gay bars and nightclubs. That I was in a low-paying dead-end job didn't help my fashion budget any.

If A.R. had lost interest in me, what did that make me? In those days I was a skeleton. I felt haggard from wanting so much. His name was a mantra that I fingerspelled at night. Hope was the last of what I had of my flesh still clinging to my bones.

Living in the West Village meant that I could visit A Different Light, a LGBTQ bookstore, on Eighth Avenue and scope out its gay poetry section more often. It was there that I found a copy of Michael Lassell's collection *Decade Dance*. The book contained a few "how-to" poems, but one in particular devastated me: "How to Watch Your Brother Die." Thus inspired, I wrote "How to Fall for a Deaf Man," which continues to be updated with each reprint to acknowledge the latest technological advances in communication.

Many of Lassell's elegies shared tender moments throughout. I felt lost in them in the same way that I'd felt lost in my hopeless love for A.R. It gradually dawned on me that my poems for A.R. were not love poems at all. They were actually elegies!

I was in perpetual mourning.

Then I finally left the advertising agency for a new job elsewhere. I couldn't stand seeing him unexpectedly and feeling so haunted.

By then I had met someone else. But that's a story for another time.

When Lawrence Schimel of A Midsummer's Night Press accepted *Mute* for publication in 2010, he insisted on paring it down to a svelte 64 pages, and set in a fairly small type for a book sized four by six inches! After having lived so long with my various iterations of *Mute*, which had occasionally ballooned only to be streamlined again, I nevertheless blanched at the cuts he'd made. I didn't give him a hard time about it, though. I understood that the desired length was partly economical not only for cost's sake but also his desire to zero onto the Deaf gay experience.

The thirteen new poems that I've included in this second edition come from several sources. According to my deteriorating digital files (we're talking WordPerfect for DOS here), it appears that I had created at least nine different versions of *Mute* in the thirty-five years since I saw A.R. last. Combing through the digital fragments, I discovered some forgotten pieces.

To honor more of my Deaf gay friends, I've restored three old elegies (Alan Barwiolek, Sam Edwards, and Bruce Hlibok) and composed four new elegies (Sam Feliciano, Jerry Koonce, James Sharer, and Guy Wonder).

I've also included a few previously published poems, including "Mumbles," my royal kiss-off to A.R. That piece necessitated that I finally pull together my third collection. Hence: *Mute*.

For a long time I grieved for the relationship that never was. I kept loathing myself for having been so undesirable to A.R. It seemed that no one else could compare to him. But time and distance has proven to be the best healer.

If I must relive those angst-filled days of A.R. at all, I grieve for that naïve young man I once was. How so woefully misguided he had been with his loving nature, and yet how so rightly he should dare himself to love so passionately against logic and reason, only to survive it all.

If not for A.R., I would not have found my métier as a poet. I thought I had needed his approval to validate my own worth as a Deaf gay man, but I didn't appreciate how I had been blessed with an extraordinary gift amidst my emotional turbulence at the time. Without realizing it, I had earned my full confidence as a poet. In other words, if I was a poet before meeting A.R., I became a Poet after meeting him.

One could say that many of the poems included here were my attempts to recover from A.R.'s seismic gaze. With whatever imperfections I may have then and now, I hadn't believed that I could be enough for a handsome man.

Now I know better. I should never have to feel the need to impress anyone, let alone him.

I am more than good enough.

—Raymond Luczak
Minneapolis, MN

I.

> "Experience teaches us
> that silence terrifies people the most."
> —Bob Dylan

How to Fall for a Deaf Man, 2025

Do not be afraid of your face.
Move into a beam of light
in the bar. Smile openly.
Watch his hands move
quicker than strobe lights
as he surveys the crowd with his friends.
Do not think of how hard
it might be to have a casual
conversation.

When he comes across the floor,
do not ask his name with
exaggerated lip movements.
A simple "How are you" will do.
Do not feel lost
in his eyes, worn thin by years
of guessing the lip movements of strangers,
and wondering for weeks afterward
exactly what they had said.

Do not look insulted
if he takes out a small pad and pen.
Write your name clearly.
Point to him and ask with your eyebrows
his name. Watch him write it down
and feel his fingers pull yours
this way and that until he nods.

Point to him in the chest and
tell him with your face, *You are cute*.
Ignore how much you are sweating.

Watch the tips of his fingers slip
off his chin and his lips mouth the word "cute."
Feel an erection coming on when he points
to you and signs, *Cute*.
Watch him write on the pad, *You are
very nice to ask*. Nod again,
not because you don't know what to say,
but because you don't know the signs.

Ask to exchange text numbers.
Try not to feel amazed by the speed of his typing.
Let the glow of the tiny screens
illuminate each other's faces
in the darkness surrounding you.

Do not feel embarrassed when
you ask, "How do you say, Thank you?"
Repeat the question. Do
not feel frustrated when he shakes
his head no. Do not type furiously
on your phone, *How do you say thank you?*
Watch him sign, *Thank-you*. Follow his hand
and again until he signs, *You're-welcome*.

Realize how much elegance hands can possess.
Do not ask him the sign for *fuck*.
He is tired of showing how. He wants
sincere attempts to talk.
Do not ask him to tutor you for free.
He is not a teacher. He's tired of teaching.

Ask him where you can take sign language classes.
Try not to be bothered by his wary eyes.
You are just another one who says
he wants to learn, but never gets around to it.

Do not be startled by how
much eye contact he requires.
Do not be afraid of his face.

Do not feel surprised
when you call him later on the voice relay service
and find how clearly you understand him.
Try to feel comfortable with telling a complete stranger,
a woman's voice you will never hear again,
how much you miss him while listening
to the sound of her hands softly tapping each other
while she signs to him on the videophone.
Wait a minute's eternity before she returns with,
"I'm so happy that you called …"

Practice fingerspelling license plates,
store names, and TV program titles.
Remember to keep your palm out.
Do not think like *t-h-i-s*,
but as one word, *this*.

Watch one video after another online
showing Deaf people signing.
Try not to feel lost and overwhelmed
by what you cannot decode.
Turn off the volume when you watch
their expressions inflecting their signs.
Allow the mystery of their hands to fill your dreamery.

As you drive home alone, notice how rhythmic
telephone poles and corner signs are.
Wonder why no one ever thinks of making music
for eyes alone.

Try not to feel left out at parties
when his friends sign quickly to each other.
When he introduces you to them, say,
Nice meet you. Try not to feel
overwhelmed if you cannot read their names.
Ask again until you get their names right.
Try not to resent it when he says you are
hearing.

Keep a mask of indifference when your friends say,
never talking to his face,
"Oh, he's so cute, I mean, really,
you two are getting along?"
Watch Dinner Table Syndrome in action.
Count how many of your friends
return your texts, your calls to get together again.

Attend foreign movies and hold his hand secretly.
Learn not to whisper or demand his eyes.
Learn instead to enjoy the clarity of subtitles.
Realize that was how he'd always watched TV
and movies: foreign films without captions.

Read a few books on deafness. If he doesn't know
which ones are good, ask
his Deaf friends. Ignore the longing in their eyes
when they see how serious you are.

Realize how few hearing men have Deaf lovers.
He is a very lucky man to have you.
But do not protect him.

Allow him to fumble with his speech
when he points out his choices on the menu.

Never yell his name. Do not

lash out when he doesn't turn around
as you repeat, "Can you get over here?"
Instead, touch him gently on the shoulder.
Sign, *Yell-yell not mean. Me sorry*.
Watch him kiss your hands in forgiveness.

Observe how hearing people prefer to text
and watch captions in noisy bars.
Watch how they rarely use their voices
as they stand around, awaiting
a glance to light up their souls.

Do not worry whether you should
continue buying CDs or downloading music
or listen to the radio in the morning.
Your ears and voice are a gift
as much as his eyes and hands are.

Discover how much water and sun love takes
to grow, and how much can sprout in your hands.

Mannequins

They stand around us, barely moving,
always talking about us Deaf men—
our language of hands flickering like Zippos—
with friends, trying to hear above the loud music,
amidst drafts of beer and wafts of musk.

Alone by the wall, they conceal emotion;
a grin could break their perfect makeup of macho.
Our hands have made us too distracting
for display purposes. We wouldn't sell
even with our perfectly sculpted figures.

They tilt their leather caps, their brows in shadow.
Watching us, they remember how they used to be,
how they once never cared what others thought.
How sweet it is to shatter their porcelain faces
into pieces each time we kiss. They're sold.

Guesswork

His glances jackhammered
my heart's concrete.

His kisses were a constant fizz.
I couldn't stop uncorking.

His fingers purred across my back like cat's
tails, whispering night.

His tongue rumbled thunder.
I tasted lightning.

His mumbles braked a screech
where I stood confused.

His face erased our blackboard.
I crumbled into chalk dust.

Hearing Your Voice for the First Time
for Brian Keith Mexicott (1961–1996)

When you called, I listened,
the line between us
taut, about to snap.
We were silent, our long distance
time ticking away.

I strained to understand
your utter- ances
with my hearing aids.

Who knew a voice
thick with want could sound so

thin?

You laughed nervously
at my weak one- liners.
My mind was stripped.

That night I dreamed
of you speaking

clearly,
the timbre of your voice
sun-lit in my hands.

Pitch

Cups of tea undulated steam between us
as we sat and crept closer than ever before.
Desire caffeinated throughout our veins.

I pumped up the volume of laughter
in your eyes and what little symphony I could
hear of your voice conducting stories.

I had explained the science of my hearing.
Partially broken nerve endings. Lipreading.
Speech therapy. Technological inadequacies.

You finally stopped. "*Mea culpa*," you joked
once you caught that I couldn't follow everything.
Your face sang the full orchestra of regrets.

"Me what?" I repeated. "Oh, no,
you don't quite understand." You sighed.
"Never mind—it's not that important. Sorry."

Your averted eyes dropped a few octaves
of our initial bright choruses
until I could no longer feel your silence:

an empty chair, a tip of quarters on the table,
a half-hearted promise to keep in touch,
and a day wasted wondering why I even bother.

Hands of Moon

If only I could have my freckled skin and the slight bags under my eyes concealed in a lather of makeup so skillfully done that I would never look made up but flawless like Marlene Dietrich with the lazy curl of her cigarette smoke garlanding her face as she looks upward to the heavens of an arc light furiously hot upon her in the dark shadows of a movie theater filled with dreamers watching her and not wanting to extinguish their own cigarettes. My hands, like hers touching as if ready to break free of her face while I flicker-sign to those still wondering whether I existed in flesh, would be full of moon and immortal.

Repetitions

Tired of asking, "What was that again?"
I turn silent in their smoky presence.
I sit in the bar and stare at those men.

I am alone on Saturday night. Again.
Drink is a bitter solace; I have no defense,
tired of "Well, what did you say, then?"

I watch them nod their heads and laugh when
others throw whispers to fuel that suspense.
I sit in the bar and stare at those men.

Strobe lights strike lasers on those men
chatting. I maintain a mask's pretense,
tired of asking "What was that again?"

Silence and I are old childhood friends;
I turn off my hearing aids. My intense
eyes roam the bar and stare at those men.

They do not acknowledge me at all when
they leave with someone else. Again.
I sit in the bar and stare at those men,
who've tired of asking, "What was that again?"

Instructions to Hearing Persons Desiring a Deaf Man

His eyebrows cast shadows everywhere.
You are a difficult language to speak.

His long beard is thick with distrust.
You are another curiosity seeker.

His hands are not cheap trinkets.
Entire lives have been wasted on you.

His face is an inscrutable promise.
You are nothing but paper and ink.

His body is more than a secret language.
Tourists are rarely fluent in it.

His eyes will flicker with a bright fire
when you purge your passport of sound.

Let your hands be your new passport,
for he will then stamp it with approval.

A Deaf man is always a foreign country.
He remains forever a language to learn.

Waiting for You to Learn Sign Language

Bones in my fingers have crumbled into sand.
I am a shattered hourglass on the beach.
My cracked eyes see everything jagged.
I am afraid to touch, bleed.
The bald sun squints hard into my soul,
a pyre of empty prayers and sheaves of notes
never sent. Oceans were never this dry.
Sharks have stopped struggling in the pits.
Water has died. Each sweat bead is precious.
My skin is seared with salt crystals.
My scraped knees burn as I crawl deeper down
to the mucky bowl of crisp kelp and rotting fish.
The sea is barren. I see belly dancers
waving their hips and snapping their finger cymbals
in the distance of murmur. I'm going mad.
Everyone and everything has died. No moisture.
My chapped feet drag crimson trails behind.
The sky is clear. No birds. Just a wind-up clock
hiccupping its final tics on the other side
of the earth. Silence has lost its volume.
The sound of my weak heartbeat is thunderous.
Love, open your hands. You are a corked geyser.

One Day When I Lose My Speech

Nerve endings deep inside my ears will shrivel up
like coleus plants starved of water too long.
My speech will wither.
All that will be left: my fertile hands.

Fields of sunflowers will cascade like creeks
tumbling back into the ocean of my hands.
I will sprinkle kisses of rain across their faces.
I will stay green in times of drought.

Buildings taller than the Tower of Babel will collapse
into folding chairs when I describe them
with quick lines more accurate than blueprints.
Scale will not intimidate me. I will be an architect.

Melody will not be what it used to be. Rhythm,
come serenade me back into your arms
under a canopy of cherry trees in full blossom.
My bare feet will still feel the waft of dance.

Streets with no names will be filled with landmarks
far more distinctive, like a beauty mark.
Who needs GPS when I'm a homing pigeon?
The cartography of the lost will be my only map.

Research alone will not save my ears from dying.
Spoken words tumble like dead leaves

in the wind. Stars will fall like sugar into my hands.
Everything my hands gather will be mine.

II.

"Silence is the most intolerable of answers."
—Mason Cooley

Murmurings

Mailboxes on every corner murmur,
baby birds opening their mouths for worms,
waiting for me to drop in those letters
to you. My words slither down their throats.
Still they wail for more. How can I provide
if you've never heard the trills of my desire?
I compose you nothing but mating calls.

These babies will grow fat on what I starve
on these arpeggios of lush silence.
My ears discern every camouflaged sound,
thinking again that you've flown in to court,
only to find that you've already twittered.
Was that a postmark of yes, or no?
Nights of waiting and listening are Hell.

Buddies
for my Deaf client with AIDS, d. 1990

You never said much. You lay, blank-eyed,
under the white sheets as I
asked you questions in our common denominator
of Sign. How was I to know that later
you'd send me away, wanting to die

alone? I did stop by, didn't I?

I sat opposite you, your eyes
brightening when I became your waiter.

You never said much
when I sneaked in, on the sly,
those chocolate donuts you'd craved. I
was left with one last question when, later,
you ranted against your doctor, a traitor.
You never returned my calls. You'd become a hater
of those who could speak. Wasn't I an ally?
You'd never said much.

In the Pawnshop
for Alan R. Barwiolek (1952–1996)

Life on the bedside table cannot be
measured. You are now a broken clock,
tossed into a box readied for pawning.
Your sentimentality is suddenly cheapened.
What would the pawnshop make of you?
No longer ticking, you have no value.

The tears of rust have streaked in the dark.
The numbers have thinned your cheeks.
Your hands of time are now ashes,
a silvery baby's powder—what time was it?
In the pawnshop you end up with the freebies.
Dust collects on your tired eyes.

In your hollow skull of broken parts,
you remember. Time was a beautiful thing.
There were so many others like you,
lined up like a toy store before a big sale.
Yet you cast a charming Swiss precision.
Everyone adored you and clamored for more.

In the pawnshop you are ignored like the rest.
Everywhere are price tags of souls gone too soon.
I cup your ashes and blow them off my palms.
They sail like comets splintering with seeds
cracking the floor in half, taking root underneath.
The earth turning is a relentless clock.

Covent Garden: Men's Room, 1889

Next time you saw me outside the theatre, you dropped
a note. I picked it up, yet another coal remnant.
Light and bright as smoke-free air, I *understood*.
That I was deaf-and-dumb didn't matter.
In the deep clasp of your arms
I become a cleaned pearl cameo.
Your unbroken skin against my coarse
fingertips feels like taking off gloves
each time I touch. You
don't seem to care that my finger-
nails are crescents of black soot,
souvenirs from sweeping chimneys every day.
I groom the ends of your moustache
with the comb of my tongue,
and you wipe the rouge of soot off my face before
you sweep your tongue down my throat,
hungry, these the walls of lust,
the choked chimney of my neck.
You have no use for my hands except
for our common language of pent-up relief.
Our bodies are now ears, listening
to the cheap stalls surrounding us.

Food for Thought

The wheeing noise in the restaurant
sublimates itself into vague anecdotes
drifting between you and the Deaf man.
He is not yet twenty-one, and you are
old enough to be his father.
His nasal voice and his blue-gray eyes
are more confident than before; your lips
ache for that warmth from a Salem cigarette.
His hearing aids are turned up. Just so
he won't miss your syllables.

You watch his eyes as he eats. He must think
of you as the maestro of your past, your life, your future.
But your mouth rewrites your mind, snapping his
    hopeful baton
in two. Your dismal holidays. Your wilting mother.
Your boozy fears. So young,
how could a kid possibly understand? No.
Not in front of these people.
They are eating, enjoying themselves.
There is no need to cry. Not yet.
You act nonchalant
but your eyes are careful, measured.

He stops for a different hunger.
He is eating your words for food. But
this, a harvest of emptiness: He nods.

His smile frightens you a little—hasn't he
comprehended what you're trying to say?

You and he leave the place, weaving north
toward his bus stop on 18th Street. As you glance back
at him, you wonder
what he is really, *really* thinking.

Later
for Richard Chenault (1957–1995)

Your voice translated me,
a lucid memory.

You videotaped my hands, words.
Now that's all gone to the birds.

What led you to sign, to grasp?
Your fluency made me gasp.

You turned deaf to others' sneering.
Your ears were so used to hearing.

Translate me one more time.
I loved how we could rhyme.

Death's a cruel interpreter:
Nothing translates for later.

Wink
for John "Buzzy" Bautista Conterio (1946–1988)

How can I explain the seeming insignificance of you
in light of all that had gone before? You stared once, twice
when I was eighteen. I was so afraid,
so stilled, I never let on. But if you knew, well ...
Why didn't you? I would've liked your salt-and-pepper stubble,
a coarseness against my red beard, an entwining of sweaty fingers.
We would've wrestled madly the scent of desire out of each other
with your two spotted dogs roving outside your bedroom door.
Instead, we continued talking and ... Oh, nothing.
I wish more than anything to see you wink just one more time.

In June

As I stroll Barrow Street, blossoms everywhere remind
    me:
June will soon arrive, and then everything will break,
no longer doe-eyed, into a canopy of green. I'd feel
like dancing starry-eyed, the fool I am, into the arms
of a man. His black tufts of chest hair would soon
sprout like daisies out of his polo shirt, blowing

trumpets to romance. We'd hold hands amidst breezes
    blowing
and whistling near my hearing aids as he shows me
a lone purple crocus stretching petals—so soon?—
behind an iron tree fence. Our braiding of arms
would lead to a too-long kiss before a car horn breaks
our segue. The gawks of tourists will remind us to feel

that precariousness of wanting to feel
again, our sticky thighs cooling from winds blowing
into my bedroom, comparing sweat beads on our arms,
and chuckling at his clumsy gestures at me.
With my tie loosened during my lunch breaks,
I will watch crowds of pigeons among bread crumbs
    soon

searching for more while my notebooks would soon
fill up with *him*: his fingers never ceasing to feel
my quivering body, his tongue smoothing my breaks

of impatience, his opinions always blowing
my mind ... He'd be my muse, thrilled he could inspire me
with his caresses. And how he'd skitter into my arms,

bemoaning the trials of work that day. My arms
would calm his awkward signing, his frustrations soon
forgotten. He'd cover my neck with kisses, turning me
hard once again in the kitchen. Then at night we'd feel,
with our hairy legs crossed, a wind blowing
past goose pimples while we'd chat idly as a break

between spurts of lovemaking. Then stars would break
suddenly through my windows; with his thick arms
folded, he'd fall asleep to Coltrane blowing
notes while I dreamed of turquoise waters. But soon
we'd have to shave our stubble off for work. We'd feel
the same angst for our jobs as he says *G'bye* to me.

Ah yes, soon it will be June! That time to break
winter's wait, his arms clinging while I feel
those breezes rushing in, blowing, awakening me.

Night Stroll in Washington, D.C.

Nights once felt like years
when I was young in this old neighborhood.

Houses haven't changed, shoulders huddling
next to each other, their window eyes shut.
They've seen too many secret longings.
The brick sidewalks are bruised
from winters of feet unwilling to surrender.

Your eyes once hummed summer prairie.
I lit up with sun and forget-me-nots.

A year of wonderings passed between us.
Our words were tentative like seedlings.
The last time I saw you at the gallery,
I threw away the last of my bouquets.
There was nothing left to compost.

I moved away with not a good-bye.
But this city keeps calling me back.

With a snowy shroud on my shoulders,
I whispered wisps of warm air:
Was I too skinny for you? Too Deaf?
Or did you desire only black men?
Or was I simply too young for you?

You'll always remain a mystery.
Fifteen years passed is a season.

Your beard's gone. You've lost some hair.
You've lost weight. You walk slower.
I hear cancer's eaten away your liver.
I no longer see your beaten face,
or the man whose body I stared at.

You've become a dull ache in my bones.
Years now pass like nights.

The Loom
for André Pierre Pellerin (1958–2024)

Your thick legs, warm,
braid in and out of mine
as our hands treadle words. Our bed
is a loom, our bodies the warp and woof
in ever-changing patterns,
kisses wrapping loose strands
like language weaving
inside our hands
deftly.

III.

"Silence remains, inescapably, a form of speech."
—Susan Sontag

The Elegist

When someone dies, he is asked.
Death is too easy a task.
Clichés are brought on display,
like uncorked vintage Chardonnay.

Tears drop into rivers that never
stop. He conjures poems so clever;
his lines echo past the sad ones.
Hadn't he loved like they had once?

A few words of comfort—well, anything.
The pretense is much too emptying.
Love is an urn waiting to overflow.
Death can't be an excuse to glow.

What's left to live, and to tell?
He remembers only too well.

Algae
for Jack Leo Fennell (1948–1992)

The lesions in your brain are growing like algae
in this tank. Your life has been reduced
to wide-eyed glances darting this way and that
in Room 808 at the bustling motions, blurry
but undeniably real, through the glass.

You wonder how you ended up, here, in this tank,
dependent on the IV pump, the oxygen tube.
So many of your friends have fallen away,
no longer peering through the glass.
They've quarantined themselves in isolation tanks.

The glass walls are empty except for the clock up there.
Its ticking hands burn in your brain,
deeper than the lesions found in last week's X-rays.
Its spread is the deepest gravel of them all,
crumbling into particles angrier than salt.

You swim this way or that under the ultraviolet light,
still clear-eyed in your memories. Wasn't
it sweet, having that fourth-floor walkup
on Christopher Street, easy to scoop up men
off the street and whisk them up the stairs?

Wasn't it magical, gathering together
a posse of Deaf gay friends in discos and bars,
poppers promising the scent of everything?

So many beautiful men shimmered, shirtless
under that disco ball, while Donna Summer sang.

Your left side's paralyzed, your left arm
hot and cold, and your right arm's weak.
Even the heater can't calm your temperature.
You take in water from a Styrofoam cup,
but your lips remain impossibly parched.

You're tired of being tested over and over again,
just to make sure your pH is balanced.
You've been reduced to wearing diapers.
The alkaline stares suffocate. A nurse
found the IV tube wrapped around your neck.

But no, it wasn't tight enough. You are
still breathing, and your parents are coming
soon, and your body is again slagging with pain,
and your hand tries to sign something,
and your mind is fixated … Where are you?

Your eyes flounder from one corner to another,
your body a tank of toxins and sewage.
You close your eyes once more, praying
you never have to navigate again.
The sweet warm-bodied ocean is waiting: *Go.*

A Friendship Never Meant
for Bruce Michael Mackintosh Hlibok (1960–1995)

What? Another one going soon?
Why, it's only the end of June.

Fifth Avenue is purple screaming
with lush and pink confetti streaming.

The party seems hardly changed,
but my heart's rearranged.

You ignored me all these years,
as if I had perfect ears.

You were also a Deaf gay writer,
but you had to be a real fighter.

After you performed in *Runaways*
on Broadway, you had to snub. No praise.

But you were just seventeen!
Have you since then made the scene?

You wrote, produced, and directed a play
or two. Then I moved to New York one day.

I wanted us to be good friends
and go out on a few mindbends.

But, no, you were too good for me.
Our few talks are soon a memory.

Oh, people said all sorts of things,
and that you were tired of nothings.

Was I a nothing in your eyes?
Glances away lent truth to your lies.

Was I too "hearing" for you?
Or was I too headstrong, too true?

I made some progress in my work,
but you still acted like a jerk.

Come on, let's be friends, Bruce!
What have you got to lose?

I get a call on my TTY machine.
You're dead. It's obscene.

International Deaf Leather, 2002
for Clayton L. Valli (1952–2003)

The last time I saw you, you were
a slim white-haired daddy
sporting a crewcut and a leather vest.
I imagined the tired cigarette smoke
wafting the smell of male hunger,
drifting into the crotch of your hands,
waiting for the familiar language
of tongues and eyes unwavering,
of strange desires best not shared
in front of others trying to translate.

The first time I saw you, you were
a curly-haired professor in a polo shirt,
letting forth an eyeful of imploding
images and lines that would fail
written poetry if set down into English.
My eyes gulped down that whiskey
of signs I never had growing up.
I drank in your supple hands,
but your flask was much too slender.
I kept clicking my parched tongue for more.

Since then, eighteen years of men have passed.
Sitting next to you at the leather contest, I saw
your eyes shining quiet admiration
at this or that hunky contender
as they appeared onstage, all basking

in a sweat of nervousness. I sat a tourist
hung over, still, like that first understanding
awakened years ago when I first saw
the controlled dignity of your handshapes
never sweating poetry but intoxicating love.

Blueprinted
for Guy Charles Wonder III (1945–2020)

You told me
so many stories:
how you'd dressed
department store windows,
how you modeled,
how you left
New York City
(not daring to
glance back once
you drove west
for San Francisco
over the bridge
because you knew
you'd break down
then and there)
because you couldn't
handle more friends
dying every day,
how you struggled
with being a
HIV-positive Deaf gay
man, how you
pushed hard to
make art—*anything!*—
how you refused
to try AZT
after observing how

your friends had
died much faster
after taking it.

*

Your body
seemed built
with 2x4s.

Your mustache
grizzled beads
of sweat.

Your gaze
nailed me,
an amateur.

You blueprinted
my layout
of desire.

You took
full measure
of me:

Sign-fluent,

HIV-negative,
much younger,

currently partnered,
struggling writer,
New Yorker.

You intuited
my foundation
wouldn't be

strong enough
to leave
him behind.

Your hands
swallowed mine,
a mouth

with no
tongues wrestling,
entombing me.

1,549 Miles Away
for James Thomas Sharer (1964–2007)

This morning I thought of you lying there in the glare
of light illuminating your body covered in white.
Your neck has become another wound, a new scar
bandaged and stitched together like my heart.
You can't possibly become another number.

This afternoon I saw an older man weeping
on his way out of a Walgreens drugstore.
In his hands was a pharmacy bag of pills.
I didn't know his story, but I understood
the story of his tears, like I don't know
the story of your thick bull's neck,
its skin lightly freckled and creamy
to my tongue, my beard, my hands.

This evening I dreamed I licked your new scar like a cat
bathing itself, keeping itself clean, purring
my tongue until you finally fell asleep,
only to reawaken in the cathedral of my arms,
its stained-glass windows breathing color.

Uncloseting, 1984
for Jerry Glynn Koonce II (1962–1995)

Wearing a bouquet of fresh curls
atop his head, he perched
a pair of owl glasses on his nose
as I sat opposite him
in the lobby of Benson Hall.

He stayed upright
with the collar of his polo shirt,
green with its pink alligator
poised to snap, upturned
as he looked intently at me.

I was a gawky small-town boy
in a T-shirt and jeans.
He crossed his hairy legs,
his right foot tapping the air:
You. You. You.

In Elephant Walk, 1994
for Samuel Feliciano (1957–1995)

Mere minutes after we met,

he signed simply in ASL:

Me h-i-v positive.

Death future accept.

His smile was serene.

I was stunned.

I don't recall what I'd said

although I tried my best

to hide the gut punch

of a Deaf gay stranger

informing me without ado,

as if he expected me

to remember him

decades after the fact.

How I wanted to hold him

so fiercely so my heat

could scorch that ice out-

come right out of his bones.

I never knew him at all.

Why did he tell *me*?

What was his story?

How did he end up there

in San Francisco?

Each time I visit the Castro,

I still honor that calm angel

awaiting his wings.

The Purpose of Astronomy
for Samuel Edwards (1941–1989)

If an eye's shimmer could inspire, then please
do not take him away. Reward him
with immortality.
                    His voice has shrunk
to vivid mouse eyes and to bony fingers
too tired to sign his next word. Even his skull
leans precariously under his cap.
                            I remember
his unerring smile as he fingerspelled my name:
"R-a-y-m-o-n-d?" He could match name with face,
a born astronomer pointing out constellations.
From his wry telescope he did not tell anyone
of his discovery: my loneliness.
                            A dream
of him arose, this: no longer skeletony or vomity,
he was a solid Zeus beckoning with thunderclaps.
Past rows of charring incense and feasting tables,
I walked a dazed soul toward him.
                            His smile
faded when I flung down wine jugs, wracked with sobs.
His guests rumored my identity, my past. But
he rubbed my shoulders ...
                    Oh, how could I adore him?
We never had any chance to consummate. The rituals
of asking a man to bed still seemed unworthy of him.
Now emptied, I fell asleep beside his sandals.

                                        A sensation
awakened me with its slow traveling
along the length of my body: His mustache tickled
kisses around my nipples.
                    I laughed,
my hands wanting to ask, talk, share—
but I lost the language.
                    For he had spiraled
upward into the skies, suddenly painted night.
A thousand shimmers shone.

Marenisco Eyes
for John "Buzzy" Bautista Conterio (1946–1988)

My passport is from Michigan's Upper Peninsula.
You went into exile at the age of 18.

Twenty-five years later we traded names in ASL.
You lit up when I told you of my homeland.

"You're from Ironwood?" I nodded.
"I'm from Marenisco. Thirty minutes southeast."

In that one moment, you turned young again,
your face a pristine land awaiting discovery.

Our eyes sang the language of summers
roaming freely in the woods,

past deer droppings, fox prints,
strawberry patches, partially-eaten rabbits.

Alone, each of us daydreamed ourselves superheroes
against boys who'd thought our ears defective

enough to warrant their super powers of mockery.
In winter, we pulled caps over our ears

as we dove into the white, down the hills.
Those boys screamed and spun as

they died a thousand imaginary deaths.
We had hardened in their gulag of glances

and of dirty jokes that we couldn't lipread.
Dreaming revenge was the only way we kept warm.

We learned to keep quiet as mice,
counting the seasons' rosary beads

until the day we would grow up and leave
the cradle of the woods behind those boys.

Our eyes had taught us how to translate the seasons.
In exile we dreamed in that lost language.

Miracles did shimmer everywhere no matter the day.
One only had to know where to look.

Even a square foot of soil was rich with history,
species and smells commingling in struggle.

Somewhere in our former homeland
there must be other expatriates like us,

who've mastered the pain of distance,
knowing that blood alone isn't family enough.

One day, when I'm dead, you will hand back
my passport, welcoming me home.

You Died Today
for Robert Louis Sisco (1952–2004)

You died today, and I feel dead and buried.
You stood, a figure in black on bar nights.
You never shared words about love,
nor about those who slipped away in the mornings,
a time easy enough to find reasons to leave.
You said you always had a good time
on the nights you prowled these places.
I was never strong enough for the hunt.
Patience was your stronger suit.

I never knew whom you'd loved, or if they
loved you back with clumsy hands,
trying to learn signs, as you spoke into their ears
amidst the smoky pulse of trance music,
and fondled the thick beer bottles
you sipped from to still your loneliness. Somehow
I knew the dark valley of glances would swallow
you alive just as you would kiss a man
with a perfect set of muscles.

I've stopped wondering what will happen
to these lean strangers flickering in the strobe
lights, all waiting for *something*.
I wonder, now, how you explained away
your hearing aids, your hands, your loneliness
to strangers peering into your eyes,
windows of a strange house they'd never seen

before. I barely knew you.
Words fail when hands alone bleed.

IV.

> "The most eloquent silence;
> that of two mouths meeting in a kiss."
> —Anonymous

On a Bench with Him in Central Park

Not to acknowledge that the heart still clings
like moss, a sapling quaking in the shadow
of an oak tree, that movement of grace.
I wave with futility in his shadow,
knowing we share only the same soil, but never
equally the minerals: how sweet it would be
to share a telepathy, to comprehend instantly
the every why of his actions, the acknowledgement
that he was young once. O the need to entangle
roots, to create a history of rings together:
The heart is tenacious with its few roots.

Mute

Even the tools of my writing trade can collapse
into a broken English, a pidgin language
in which the perfect opener, witticisms, always fall
flat.

The immutability of your face has cast a spell,
a montage of "What?" and repetitions. My hands wish
    to fly
free of my voice, not caring any more whether you
    understand: Just like
that.

This lightheadedness must be hidden for fear of
    frightening
you again. (*No, not like that night when I asked you ...*)
    Oh, if I could
beckon you closer, to hear your question
what.

Homily

Take this hand: I am yours,
loincloth, nasal voice, broken ears all.
My fingers tremble against your chest.
Your sighs are a hymn in rhyme.
Sweet blood aches against us.
Look not away from my eyes, peering
deeper than amens barely felt.
The blessing air between us is a prayer.

This hand unlocks a communion of mouths
leaping, catching, savoring.
Our wine of sweat and saliva is not red,
a miracle of holy clarity.
Rest not in your pursuit of mad heresy,
of what next in you will implode.
Please. Listen not to what I preach.
May our bodies become Scripture.

Audiological Exam

First, a tender beep, a raising of hand
mirrored against the double-paned windows.

A staccato mutter, a pair of averted eyes.
Sometimes nothing. Doubts echoed.

Cochlea, a French horn, pressed its keys
entangled in the skein of nerve yarns.

Half-knitted notes tumbled out.
Remnants of a quilt yet stitched.

Closed eyelids a blanket of quiet.
Him and his legs draped across me.

That clear tone of his moans, stilled.
My soul, cushioned between headphones.

Gazes

A noise:
gazes of strangers whiplash as one,
a school of fish changing directions,
heading that-a-way
until another noise

>snaps their eyes
>elsewhere.
>I shimmer along
>their waves of sound,
>monitoring.

Where your eyes point
that sound, I follow,
the quicksilver that I am,
hoping that you will
return to me,

>a glint of nickel
>in a sea
>of undulating krill.

A Wish, Unheard

Once I saw him sitting in his crowded office from a new
 distance.
Co-workers were laughing, giggling almost, beside his
 huge window:
A view of the world grew shimmering through the
 morning glass.
There were the usual skyscrapers, throngs of shoppers,
 impatient cars.
As with anything else, he'd ceased to notice; it had
 always been his.
He doubled over in laughter while others tossed in
 more jokes.
He did not have to lipread or ask for a rewind: I wanted
 to sliver
off my ears—forgetting I could catch only so much—
 and
give him my bloodied ears on a satin pillow and say,
 Here. All
this is my life.

Couplets
for William M. Hoffman (1939–2017)

From birth to death, we learn to couple:
the groping for something supple

in dark movie theaters, petting,
to affairs in cheap motel settings ...

Why must our faces convey distance
when we long to be touched, for instance?

Such hormones hold us in sway,
torment us when, alone, we lay.

Is it through the act we hope
to be happy? Is that how we cope

with that abyss
of loneliness?

Sometimes we misunderstand our need
to connect: the most human creed.

1989

1.

My headphones blast melodies
that I barely decipher. A voice from the past
sings of being haunted by the dead.
In my hands are whispers of lyrics I once sang
in my mind's voice. I no longer remember
what I swore to be catchy hooks.
I was never a one-hit wonder.

2.

In the darkening forest,
a single orange mushroom shone
gleaming and gloating
swift in the short distance
from the woman heavy with gauze
standing next to a shiny suitcase,
waiting for the train to materialize.

3.

Rising up in the elevator,
I stand my corner, alone
while a diamond ring rose up in the air,

a feather in reverse,
a half-carat from its brief union
shared in the Bahamas
and discarded over a single
cell phone call hiccupping
in static breaths.

I try to catch it,
but it too is a kiss of yours,
already evaporating.

4.

Sitting a few offices away from you
was sweet torment. Each fitful night
brought you forth in your many guises.
No matter the fantasy, I recognized
the stare of hunger I starved for.

I hadn't mastered the language of ache.
I was still illiterate,
having been taught not to expect
affection. Poverty was all I'd known.
That you even looked my way made me
feel like a billionaire
smoking a Havana cigar in a Jacuzzi.

5.

One dawn I woke up face-down
in the cold peat, shivery from the rain
the night before. My translucent eyelids,
now windows to the few millimeters
of dark and moist, revealed
an orgy of worms sheathing and unsheathing
toward the first kiss of sun.

6.

Third Avenue seems a century ago,
a country I'd visited far too quickly,
not knowing that my passport wasn't due to expire
anytime soon. I was so afraid of deportation.

The sidewalks where we once walked
are still there. Our invisible footprints
have long been carpeted with others
trampling upward on the career ladder.
Some, I'm sure, have fucked on the office couch,
docking merit pay. I chose not to sue you.
My heart wanted sexual harassment
and win your heart handily in court.

7.

In the full moon's discerning cast,
the rose garden off Lake Harriet,
its colors lined up and sagging,
is filled with specters who claimed
to know sign language once upon a time.

I walk among these liars. They do not wave
for my attention. My eyes are clear
amidst what they think are signs.
They give poor imitations of a secondhand language.
My hands are not a thrift shop made for ransacking.

I once wept a year over the perfection
of your sculpted hands never lying
when you copied the flowers blooming
out of my hands. Your smiling eyes
watered each tendril of vine I grew.
You were a wall I had to scale.

8.

Beneath the sagging collapse of the 35-W bridge,
the sludge of Mississippi River is lined
with bodies that must be found at all costs.

The divers do not dwell on the fact
that many more dead bodies have decayed
decades before in the peat-heavy beds. Their bones,
worn down to nubs in the constant slurries,
are collapses never reconstructed. They are only stories
never repeated after their grieving loved ones die.

Somewhere deep in the East River
between Manhattan and Brooklyn
is my 23-year-old body that you discarded.

The sediment is still trying to gush
remains back into the ocean.
My story isn't unique enough to be driftwood.

Long after I meet my mortality, I will sink
in the frothy foam of wave and sun.
Your arms will be wide open among the seaweeds
waving welcome where I will weep for the last time
in the bed of aches sated at last.

9.

Last night you called me in a dream.
I answered. You said things.
I laughed. You chuckled.

We agreed on our foolishness.
Then we hung up.

   10.

This year is the twentieth anniversary
of our fatal first gaze. You stranded me
at the altar the second I said, "I do."

For our honeymoon I slept with the ghost of you.
I traveled the Grand Tour of heartbreak too often.
There were never enough stickers to cover my suitcases
or enough tips to pay my hotel porters. I was rich
with the liquid blood money of my heart.
My arteries hardened anyway.

   11.

Our last phone conversation was a tennis match
of mumbles always misunderstanding.
Our scores were always 0 = Love.

I always had to turn up my hearing aids
just to hear your voice. I used to memorize
its timbre. Last night you spoke to me

in a dream. My hearing had long faded
that I didn't know it was you until
I tried to discern your mumbles.

12.

The alarm shook its finger
at me in the twilight of dream.
I see him still, the jewel who breathed
a warm heat in the empty cup
of my hands on a wintry evening.
His green eyes cast an emerald glance
across my blanketed body
that he once woven in dreams.

He once knew me when I was noon,
clear and free of shadows.
I am already midnight.
As I watch him turn away,
I purr and unravel.

Mumbles

Those eyes of white tiles will never floor me
anymore. Those restroom days are over, my dear,
when you had to hold your chin at an angle.
You are a balding statue crumbling into dandruff.
I thought you were my masterpiece.

I tear up the image of your Roman lips.
Ovid can go to hell. I plunder your face,
that treasure trove of details, for flaws.
The jewels are not worth the one year's price.
You would not sell at a pawnshop. I know.

I tried to get you to speak more clearly.
Instead you became a clapping monkey,
so charming in that blue business suit.
The elevators were a circus of glances.
I'm tired of paying for the admissions.

You are now a parrot whose voice squawks.
Tell me, who were you repeating? You sat
perched on my finger, but you only craned
for my peanuts. Your beak scrunched
their shells, and I fell in piecemeal shards.

The parquet is alive with huge roaches.
Their legs chitter like tapping fingers,
*unh-huh*s from your wheezy iron lung.

You are now a pest in the room of my eyes.
I exterminate from all corners those eggs.

I turn cold as a fridge. Inside
my heart is preserved in a Tupperware box.
It is safe from your toxic green molds.
Your eyes are a push-button microwave oven.
I have better outlets for my voltage.

I dry my hair with a blowdryer. It burns
fire in my hand, but my asbestos skin
endures the Bunsen burner of your eyes.
You are only an instrument of gas and air.
I am not a chemistry experiment.

Take note of my temperature. The year of
gray barometers under my eyes is over.
Translating the Morse code of your mumbles
almost discombobulated my compass hands.
But I've found the sea. My ship is waiting.

Orphans

Aswirl in the air like snowflakes,
family stories melt before they reach
our lost ears. We lipread what we can
around the dinner table and in cars,
connecting the dots of laughs and looks
to an imaginary sky of constellations
waiting to be explained and pointed out,
filling the missing gaps in plot twists
unfolding before our eyes. Their lives
braid and unbraid like a knitted scarf
flapping in fierce gusts of wind
while we hang on to our scarves
and stare deep into the darkening sky.

Each decibel of their laughs adds slowly
to our tinderbox that no one notices
by the fireplace. When we burst
at last into flames, they act shocked,
disbelieving that we'd count the years
of "I'll explain later" against "I'm busy
right now, can this wait till later?"
against "That's nonsense—of course,
you're family!" against "Oh, please"
against "Hearing people don't hear
everything" against "Not everything
we say is important." They never explain
when we demand, "Why say anything at all?"

When we finally stumble and find each other,
usually in the dark of night becoming
day spilling onto our shivering palms,
we gather around tables in well-lit places
and tell each other the same old stories
of how they never took time to explain
to us the spaghetti messes of their lives
all night long until we become family
deeper than blood throbbing in our hands.
Our hugs of understanding grow tighter.
Later does come, and when it does,
our laughter is a tender scrapbook
that not even they can torch.

Alan R. Barwiolek | William Bradley | Mark Branson | William D. Byrd | John "Buzzy" Bautista Conterio | Samuel Edwards | Michael Eisele | Ronald A. Emrich | Samuel Feliciano | Michael P. Felts | Jack Leo Fennell | John R. Flynn | Gerry Garrison | Bruce Michael Mackintosh Hlibok | Ernest Hoffmann | Rodney Jamison | Thomas Kane | Jerry Glynn Koonce II | J. Charlie McKinney | Cagney Savoy Perkins | Olgar Schroeder | Tommy Saavedra | Edward Schwartz | James Thomas Sharer | Robert Louis Sisco | Pedro Solis | James S. Tola | Clayton L. Valli | Mike White | Guy Charles Wonder III

Acknowledgments

A&U Magazine: "The Purpose of Astronomy."

Able-Together: "Covent Garden: Men's Room, 1889" (originally called "A London Tryst, 1889").

Bent: "Homily" and "The Loom."

Christopher Street: "Buddies" and "In June" (originally titled "June Sestina").

Creamdrops: "Food for Thought" and "Night Stroll in Washington, D.C."

The Deaf American: "Later."

Deaf Worlds 2006: HIV/AIDS and the Deaf Communities (Leila Monaghan and Constance Schmaling, eds.; Forest Publishers): "You Died Today" (originally titled "Someone Died Today").

Eyes of Desire: A Deaf Gay & Lesbian Reader (Raymond Luczak, ed.; Alyson Books): "How to Fall for a Deaf Man, 2025" (originally titled "How to Fall for a Deaf Man") and "Wink" (originally titled "Elegy for 'Buzzy' Conterio").

Eyes of Desire 2: A Deaf GLBT Reader (Raymond Luczak, ed.; Handtype Press): "International Deaf Leather, 2002" and "Pitch."

Kiss-Fist: "Gazes."

No Walls of Stone: An Anthology of Literature by Deaf and Hard-of-Hearing Writers (Jill Jepson, ed.; Gallaudet University Press): "A Wish, Unheard."

OutSight Magazine: "Murmurings" (originally titled "Coming Out").

Queer Crips: Disabled Gay Men and Their Stories (Bob Guter and John Killacky, eds.; Harrington Park Press): "Repetitions."
The Ragged Edge: "Algae" and "Mute."
The Tactile Mind: "The Elegist," "A Friendship Never Meant," and "Mumbles."
Van Gogh's Ear: "Instructions to Hearing Persons Desiring a Deaf Man."

The poem "Orphans" was a winner in the Deaf-Themed Literary Contest 2008, which was sponsored by the National Technical Institute for the Deaf (NTID)/Rochester Institute of Technology (RIT).

The poem "Instructions to Hearing Persons Desiring a Deaf Man" was selected for *Best Gay Poetry 2008* (Lawrence Schimel, ed.; A Midsummer Night's Press). It was also chosen for *Deaf American Poetry* (John Lee Clark, ed.; Gallaudet University Press). It has been adapted into a short animated film by Brooke Griffin.

I remain honored that the reviewer Amos Lassen listed *Mute* as the third best book of 2010.

I am eternally grateful to Michael Lassell for his "how-to" poems that inspired the original version of my poem "How to Fall for a Deaf Man, 2025."

Part of this book would not have been made possible without scholarship support of the Poetry Society of America. Special thanks go to Marilyn Hacker for her inspiration.

I still appreciate the joint support of my work by the Jerome Foundation and the VSA arts of Minnesota with an Artist Recognition Grant 2005.

This book could not have been completed without the assistance of the Rachel Vaughan Memorial Scholarship at the Loft Literary Center, Minneapolis, Minnesota. Tokens of eternal gratitude go to the facilitator Jude Nutter and those who provided invaluable feedback on parts of the manuscript: Denise duMaurier, John Flynn, Bart Galle, Diana Lundell, Mike McCarron, and MaryAnn Moenck. I also appreciate Vivien Luczak's assistance in verifying John "Buzzy" Bautista Conterio's years of birth and death.

As always, I remain grateful to John Lee Clark and Tom Steele (*in memoriam*) for their continued faith, Lawrence Schimel of A Midsummer Night's Press for bringing out the first edition of *Mute* back in 2010, and Eric Thomas Norris for his sharp editorial insights on this new edition. Special thanks go to Mark Ehrke for his help with the cover photograph!

For those who've cherished the 2010 edition of *Mute*, I remain forever in your debt. Thank you.

About the Author

Raymond Luczak is the author and editor of 38 titles, including *Animals Out-There W-i-l-d: A Bestiary in English and ASL Gloss*, *Ironhood: Poems*, and *I'll Tell You Later: Deaf Survivors of Dinner Table Syndrome*. His work has appeared in *Poetry*, *Prairie Schooner*, and elsewhere. An inaugural Zoeglossia Poetry Fellow, Luczak lives in Minneapolis, Minnesota. [raymondluczak.com]